IT'S TIME TO MOVE
COOKBOOK
GET OUT OF MY HOME!

"A WATCHED POT NEVER BOILS, BUT AN IGNORED POT WILL THROW A SURPRISE PARTY FOR THE SMOKE DETECTOR".

BY AMY BARROW

Contents

I   The basics

II   Easy dishes

III   Hot tips

IV   Your recipes

V   Notes

CHAPTER I
The Basics

A key life skill to have is knowing how to boil water. This will give you the foundation knowledge for a number of recipes, food and drinks. With this knowledge, you'll soon be able to cook a bowl of pasta, boil an egg, make a cup of coffee and much more.

How to boil water

Ingredients:

- ○ Water (any kind, as long as it's liquid)
- ○ Salt (optional, but recommended for flavor and health)

Items:

- ○ Kettle or a pot (whichever is handy)
- ○ Stove or an outlet (whichever is working)
- ○ Cup (or any container that can hold water)

Instructions:

Option 1: Using a kettle

1. Fill the kettle with water. Don't worry about the amount, just make sure it's enough for your needs.
2. Plug the kettle in and turn it on. Wait for the whistle or the click. If you have a fancy kettle with a temperature setting, set it to "boil" or 100°C.
3. Pour the boiling water into your cup. Be careful not to burn yourself or spill the water. You're done!

Option 1: Using a kettle

1. Fill the pot with water. Don't worry about the amount, just make sure it's enough for your needs.
2. Put the pot on the stove and turn on the heat. Add some salt if you want. Wait for the bubbles. If you have a thermometer, check if it's 100°C.
3. Transfer the boiling water to your cup. Be careful not to burn yourself or spill the water. You're done!

Warning

Boiling water is very hot (100°C). That's hotter than your coffee, your shower, or your ex. Be careful with it. Don't touch, drink, or throw it. Turn off the heat. Avoid fire, flood, or lawsuit. You have been warned!

Now that you have the skills to boil a pot of water. Let's use those skills to make some food. With two simple ingredients, water and eggs, you can create your very first meal.

Boiling an egg

Ingredients:

- ⭕ Eggs (as many as you want, not more than you can eat)
- ⭕ Water (enough to cover the eggs in the pot)
- ⭕ Salt (optional, for seasoning and preventing cracking)
- ⭕ Vinegar (optional, for easier peeling)

Items:

- ⭕ Pot with a lid
- ⭕ Stove
- ⭕ Slotted spoon
- ⭕ Bowl of cold water
- ⭕ Egg timer (or a watch, or a phone, or your intuition)

Instructions:

1. Put the eggs and water in the pot. Add salt and vinegar if you like. They will help the eggs behave and peel better.

2. Boil the water over high heat. Wait for the bubbles. This may take a while, depending on the pot and the eggs.

3. Turn off the heat and cover the pot. Let the eggs sit in the hot water for how long you want. Use a timer or your intuition. Here are some times for different eggs:
   - Soft: 4 to 6 minutes
   - Medium: 8 to 10 minutes
   - Hard: 12 to 15 minutes

4. Move the eggs to the cold water. This will stop them from cooking and burning. Let them cool for a bit, or until you can touch them.

5. Peel the eggs and enjoy them as they are, or with some toppings. You can also chop them and use them for other dishes. The choice is yours!

Warning

Boiling eggs is tricky. Watch the heat, the time, and the peeling. Too much of anything can ruin the eggs. Follow the recipe and use common sense. Don't overdo or underdo anything. And wash your hands. Salmonella is not fun. You have been warned.

Rice is the ultimate sidekick. It goes well with almost anything, from meat and sauce to veggies and spices. But how do you cook it right? Follow this simple recipe for steamed rice and you'll never go wrong. It's easy, quick, and foolproof. Just don't forget the lid. Or the water.

Cooking rice

Ingredients:

- ○ Rice (any kind you like)
- ○ Water (enough to cover the rice)
- ○ Salt (a pinch or a dash)
- ○ Oil (A drop or a drizzle)
- ○ Optional: Butter, cheese, herbs, spices, or anything else you like

Items:

- ○ Pot with a lid
- ○ Serving spoon
- ○ Stove
- ○ Bowl and fork

Instructions:

1. Wash the rice until it stops being cloudy. That means it's clean and not sticky.
2. Put the rice and water in the pot. Use twice as much water as rice. Add salt, butter, or oil if you want. They make the rice tasty, but also fatty.
3. Boil the rice and water on high heat. Then lower the heat and cover the pot. Wait for 15 to 20 minutes. Don't peek or stir. That ruins the rice.
4. Fluff the rice with a fork. Put it on a plate. Eat it with something else or by itself. Don't burn your tongue or your fingers. That hurts.
5. Add some toppings to your rice. You can use chopped scallions, toasted sesame seeds, fried garlic for some extra crunch and flavor.
6. Reheat leftover rice in a microwave or a skillet. You can also use it to make fried rice, rice pudding, or rice balls. Don't waste any rice!

Warning

Warning: Rice is yummy, but careful. Rice, water, and heat can hurt you. Water and steam can scald you if it's too hot. So, be smart and safe. Don't ruin the rice. You have been warned.

Steamed vegetables are a great staple food, a great accompaniment for meals and low in calories. Steamed vegetables are suggested to lower your cholesterol, and increase your boredom.

Steaming vegetables

Ingredients:

- ○ Vegetables of your choice, i.e. carrots, cauliflower, broccoli, zucchini, etc. (Washed and chopped)
- ○ Water
- ○ Salt and pepper, to taste
- ○ Butter or olive oil, (optional)
- ○ Lemon juice or vinegar (optional)

Items:

- ○ Pot with a lid
- ○ Steamer basket or colander
- ○ Stove
- ○ Plate or a bowl
- ○ Fork or a spoon, or your intuition)

Instructions:

1. Fill the pot with water, but not too much. You don't want to drown the vegetables. Just enough to cover the bottom of the pot. Add some salt to the water, if you like. It will make the water boil faster and give some flavor to the vegetables.
2. Put steamer or colander in pot. Not in water. Above water.
3. Put veggies in steamer or colander. Not too many. Just enough.
4. Cover pot with lid. Put pot on stove. Turn on heat. Wait for water to boil. Then wait some more.
5. Remove lid from pot. Remove steamer or colander from pot. Be careful. Hot stuff. Ouch.
6. Season veggies with salt, pepper, butter, oil, lemon, or vinegar. Whatever you like. You decide.
7. Eat the veggies on their own or to accompany a meal.

Warning

Steamed veggies can be tasty but cooking with hot water can be dangerous. Be careful not to burn yourself or overboil the water. Water can turn to steam, dry out, the pot burns and then your house. You have been warned.

Cup noodles are a delicious, easy, cheap meal to make and can also be a base for other meals. Before you jump ahead to more expert recipes, let's learn the basics.

Cup noodles

Ingredients:

- ☐ Cup noodles (any flavor, but chicken is classic)
- ☐ Water (enough to fill the cup)
- ☐ Toppings (optional, but recommended for extra flavor and nutrition)

Items:

- ☐ A kettle or a pot (to boil the water)
- ☐ A fork or a spoon (to stir and eat the noodles)
- ☐ Slotted spoon
- ☐ A napkin or a bib (to wipe your mouth and avoid stains)

Instructions:

1. Open the cup noodles and add toppings if you want. Cheese, eggs, ham, veggies, anything goes.
2. Boil the water using the kettle or the pot. You don't need to measure it, just eyeball it.
3. Pour the boiling water into the cup, up to the line. Don't burn yourself or spill the water. That's bad.
4. Close the lid and wait for 3 minutes. Use a fork or a spoon to push the noodles down. You can also do something else, like watch Netflix.
5. Open the lid and stir the noodles. Add the seasoning packet and more stuff if you like. Salt, pepper, soy sauce, whatever you fancy.
6. Enjoy your cup noodles with your fork or your spoon. Don't burn your mouth or slurp too loud. You can also drink the broth, but watch the sodium and the calories.

Warning

Cooking cup noodles is easy, but not safe. Watch the water, the heat, and the toppings. Too much water can scald you or damage the cup. Too much heat can cause a fire or an explosion. Too much toppings can make the cup overflow or spoil the noodles. So, follow the instructions and use common sense. Don't overfill, overheat, or overload the cup. And don't eat the noodles if they are bad. You don't want to get sick. You have been warned.

An underrated classic with a bad rep, beans on toast is a cheap and easy meal to make. High in protein and fibre. A meal you've bean thinking about.

Beans on toast

Ingredients:

- Bread (any kind, but whole wheat is apparently healthier)
- Butter (or margarine, or oil, or nothing)
- Baked beans (canned or homemade. Who are you kidding, it'll be canned)
- Salt and pepper (optional, but recommended)

Items:

- A toaster (or an oven, or a grill, or a fire)
- A saucepan (or a microwave-safe bowl, or a pot)
- A stove (or a microwave, or a campfire)
- A knife (or a spoon, or your fingers)
- A plate (or a napkin, or your hand)

Instructions:

1. Toast the bread with butter. You can use one or two slices. You can also cut the bread into smaller pieces.

2. Heat the baked beans with cheese, salt, and pepper. You can use the stove or the microwave.

3. Put the toast on the plate. You can use a knife, a spoon, or your fingers to spread the butter.

4. Spoon the beans over the toast. You can add more cheese, salt, and pepper if you want.

5. Enjoy your baked beans on toast. Be careful not to burn or drop anything.

Warning

Baked beans on toast is easy, but not safe. Watch the bread, the beans, and the heat. Too hard bread can hurt your teeth. Too hot beans can burn your mouth. Too high heat can cause a fire. Follow the recipe and use common sense. Don't overdo or underdo anything. And clean up after yourself. You don't want to attract ants or rats. You have been warned.

Nothing beats the crispy crunch and salty goodness of homemade potato fries. Whether you call them chips or fries, they are easy to make and hard to resist.

Hot chips / Fries

Ingredients:

- ◯ Potatoes, washed and peeled
- ◯ Oil, enough to deep-fr
- ◯ Salt, pepper, and other seasonings of your choice
- ◯ Optional: Ketchup, mayo, cheese, or other sauces of your choice

Items:

- ◯ Knife and cutting board
- ◯ Large pot
- ◯ Slotted spoon
- ◯ Baking tray
- ◯ Paper towel

Instructions:

1. Cut the potatoes into thin strips. Try to make them even. Don't cut your fingers. That's bad.
2. Heat the oil in the large pot over high heat. Be careful not to burn yourself. Or the house. That's worse.
3. Fry the potato strips in batches until golden and crispy. Don't overcrowd the pot. Or overcook the fries. That's sad.
4. Drain the fries on the paper towel. Sprinkle with salt, pepper, and other seasonings. Don't be stingy. Or too generous. That's bland. Or salty.
5. Alternative to steps 1 - 4, use a bag of frozen chips/fries and cook in the oven.
6. Serve the fries with ketchup, mayo, cheese, or other sauces. Or eat them plain. That's fine.
7. Enjoy your potato fries. They're delicious and addictive.

Warning

Potato fries are yummy, but careful. Potatoes, oil, and seasonings can hurt you. Potatoes can make you fat. Oil can make you splatter. Seasonings can make you sneeze. So, be smart and safe. Don't ruin the fries. And wash your hands because it's gross not to. Seriously, it's gross. Don't be gross. You have been warned.

Sausages are awesome! Perfect for any occasion, whether it's a cozy dinner or a backyard BBQ. They are affordable, convenient, and delicious.

Sausages

Ingredients:

- ○ Ready made sausages of your choosing, e.g. beef, pork or veggie (if you like that kind of thing).
- ○ Oil or butter

Items:

- ○ Frying pan
- ○ Stove
- ○ Tongs
- ○ Knife
- ○ Plate

Instructions:

1. Pour some oil or butter in a frying pan and heat it over medium-high heat. Don't use too much oil. You don't want to deep-fry the sausages. Just enough to make them sizzle and brown.

2. Add the sausages to the hot oil and cook them for about 15 minutes, turning them occasionally with tongs or a fork and brown all the way around. Don't get distracted and let them burn.

3. Poke then a little with a knife to release a tiny amount of the juices. You're thank me later when you don't squirt hot oil on your face or in your mouth.

4. Remove the sausages from the pan and drain the excess oil on some paper towels or a plate. Be careful not to touch the sausages or the pan with your bare hands. They are very hot. And very greasy.

5.
   - Option 1: Serve of a slice of bread with sauce, i.e., tomato sauce and mustard to your liking.
   - Option 2: Serve with steamed veggies, if you like that kind of thing. Or not. I don't judge.
   - Option 3: Serve with hot chips. Because life is too short to count calories, carbs, or kilojoules

6. Enjoy!

Warning

Sausages are yum but fatty, not that there's anything wrong with that. Just be careful of hot oil burning your face and mouth. Also be careful of splitting oil while cooking and resist the urge to eat while smoking hot. You have been warned.

Canned soup is a handy pantry staple that can be used to make a quick and easy meal. Here is a recipe for canned soup that you can customize with different flavors and toppings.

Soup

Ingredients:

- 1 can of soup of your choice. E.g. Chicken noodle, tomato, mushroom.
- Water or milk, as directed on the can. Water will make the soup thinner, while milk will make it creamier.
- Optional seasonings, such as salt, pepper, garlic powder, onion powder, or herbs.
- Optional toppings, such as cheese, croutons, crackers, bacon bits, or sour cream. These will add some texture and richness to your soup.

Items:

- Pot and stove
- Can opener
- Spoon and bowl

Instructions:

1. Open the can of soup with the can opener. Be careful not to cut yourself on the sharp edges. That's bad.
2. Pour the soup into the pot. Add water or milk according to the instructions on the can. Stir well with the spoon. You can also add some seasonings if you want. Don't go overboard, though. You don't want to ruin the soup.
3. Heat the soup over medium-high heat until it boils. Then lower the heat and simmer for a few minutes, stirring occasionally. Don't let the soup burn or boil over. That's messy.
4. Ladle the soup into the bowl. Sprinkle some toppings if you like. They will make the soup more fun and yummy.
5. Enjoy your canned soup. It's warm, comforting, and satisfying. You can also share it with someone else. Or not. It's up to you.

Warning

Canned soup is yummy, but hot. Watch the soup, the water or milk, and the heat. Too much water or milk can make the soup watery. Too little water or milk can make the soup thick. Too high heat can make the soup scorch. So, follow the recipe and use your brain. Don't mess up the soup. And wash your hands and stuff. Because, ew. You have been warned.

"REMEMBER, MASTERING THESE BASICS ISN'T JUST ABOUT IMPRESSING YOUR FRIENDS OR SAVING MONEY—IT'S YOUR TICKET TO CULINARY INDEPENDENCE AND YOUR PARENTS FINALLY RECLAIMING THEIR PANTRY!".

CHAPTER II
Easy Dishes

Roast Chicken

Ingredients:

- A whole raw chicken
- Olive oil or butter
- Ideal herbs and spices, such as garlic, rosemary, thyme, salt, pepper, paprika
- Optional: Vegetables, i.e. potato, sweet potato, pumpkin, carrot

Items:

- Roasting pan or baking dish
- Oven
- Knife

Instructions:

1. Heat oven to 190°C. Wash and dry chicken. Put chicken in pan. Add veggies if you want. Mix oil or butter with herbs and spices. Brush or spoon on chicken. Stuff lemon and herbs in chicken. Tie legs. Tuck wings.

2. Roast for 90 minutes. Check temp. It should be 150°C. Baste every 15 minutes. Cover with foil if too dark. Remove foil if too light. Do nothing if just right.

3. Rest for 10 minutes. Carve and serve. Enjoy.

4. Save the bones and the leftover meat. You can use them to make soup or stock later. Just boil them with water, salt, and more herbs and spices. Strain and store in the fridge or freezer. Waste not, want not.

5. Clean the pan and the knife. You don't want to leave them dirty. They might get rusty or moldy. That's gross. Use soap and water. Scrub well. Dry well. Put them away. Be neat and tidy.

Warning

Roast chicken is yummy, but careful. Chicken, oil, and oven can hurt you. Cook chicken well. Raw chicken can make you sick. Watch out for oil splatter. Use brush or spoon to baste. Be cautious with oven. Use oven mitts. Don't touch hot things. Be smart and safe. Don't ruin chicken. You have been warned.

Pasta, the ultimate customizable meal. Pick your shape, sauce, and toppings. Cook, mix, and serve. It's that simple. And delicious.

Pasta

Ingredients:

- ◯ Pasta, any shape you like
- ◯ Water, enough to cover the pasta
- ◯ Salt, a pinch or a handful
- ◯ Oil, a splash or a glug
- ◯ Sauce, any kind you like
- ◯ Sauce, any kind you like
- ◯ Cheese, grated or sliced
- ◯ Optional: Meat, vegetables, herbs, spices, or anything else you like

Items:

- ◯ Large pot, colander and saucepan
- ◯ Serving Spoon
- ◯ Stove
- ◯ Bowl and fork

Warning

Pasta is yummy, but careful. Pasta, water, sauce: watch out. They can be trouble. Pasta can add to your weight. Water can scald you. Sauce can choke you. Be smart and safe. You have been warned.

Instructions:

1. Fill the large pot with water and bring it to a boil. Add salt and oil. Don't be shy. Salt adds flavor. Oil prevents sticking. Or so they say.

2. Add the pasta to the boiling water and stir. Cook according to the package directions. Or until you're hungry. It's up to you.

3. Drain the pasta in the colander. Shake off the excess water. Or don't. Some people like it wet. Some people like it dry. Some people like it in between. It's your choice.

4. Heat the sauce in the saucepan over low heat. Stir occasionally. Don't let it burn. Or boil. Or splatter. That's bad.

5. Add cheese to the sauce and stir until melted. Or not. Some people like it cheesy. Some people like it saucy. Some people like it both. It's your call.

6. Add optional meat, vegetables, herbs, spices, or anything else you like to the sauce and stir. Or not. Some people like it plain. Some people like it fancy. Some people like it weird. It's your thing.

7. Serve the pasta with the sauce on top. Or on the side. Or mixed together. Or separately. It's your style.

8. Enjoy your pasta. It's delicious and filling.

Grilled cheese sandwiches are the best thing since sliced bread. Literally. They're warm, cheesy, and crispy. They're perfect for any occasion, from lunch to midnight cravings. Who doesn't love grilled cheese sandwiches?

Grilled Cheese

Ingredients:

- Two slices of bread
- Cheese (experiment with various types).
- Butter

Items:

- Frying pan
- Spatula
- Stove
- Plate and knife

Instructions:

1. Spread butter on one side of each bread slice. This will make it crispy and golden.
2. Put cheese on the unbuttered side of one bread slice. This will make it cheesy and gooey.
3. Put the other bread slice on top, buttered side up. This will make a sandwich.
4. Heat the frying pan over medium heat. This will make it hot and ready
5. Carefully place the sandwich in the pan. This will make it sizzle and melt.
6. Flip the sandwich with the spatula after a few minutes. This will make it cook evenly and avoid burning.
7. Transfer the sandwich to the plate when both sides are brown and the cheese is melted. This will make it done and delicious.
8. Cut the sandwich in half with the knife. This will make it easier to eat and share.
9. Enjoy your grilled cheese sandwich. This will make you happy and full.

Warning

A grilled cheese sandwich is yummy, but hot. Watch the cheese, the butter, and the heat. Too much cheese can make the sandwich ooze. Too much butter can make the sandwich greasy. Too high heat can make the sandwich char. So, follow the recipe and use your sense. Don't mess up the sandwich. Wash your hands, because you don't know where you've been. You have been warned.

Feel like Indian, Thai, Malaysian, etc. With this simple recipe, you can make almost any cuisine.

Meat and sauce

Ingredients:

- ◯ Meat of your choice, i.e. chicken breast, beef, pork, etc.
- ◯ Jar of cooking sauce of your choice, i.e. curry, satay, sweet and sour
- ◯ Vegetables, usually green, i.e. broccoli, beans, spinach
- ◯ Onion and garlic, chopped
- ◯ A splash of olive oil
- ◯ Rice, cooked (optional)

Items:

- ◯ Frying pan or a wok and stove
- ◯ Spatula or a wooden spoon
- ◯ Plate or a bowl
- ◯ Fork or chopsticks

Instructions:

1. Cook onion, garlic, and optional ginger, chili, or lemongrass with oil in a frying pan or a wok over medium-high heat. Stir occasionally until soft and fragrant.
2. Cook meat of your choice with optional salt, pepper, soy sauce, or fish sauce in the same pan or wok. Stir occasionally until browned and cooked through.
3. Add jar of cooking sauce of your choice and bring to a boil. Reduce the heat and simmer until thickened and bubbly. Add optional coconut milk, peanut butter, or vinegar for extra creaminess, nuttiness, or tanginess.
4. Add vegetables of your choice and cook until tender-crisp. Stir occasionally. Add optional lime juice, cilantro, or basil for extra freshness and herbiness.
5. Serve the meat and sauce dish over rice, cooked. Use a plate or a bowl, a fork or chopsticks.

Warning

Meat and sauce dish is yummy, but risky. Watch the meat, the sauce, and the heat. Raw meat can make you ill. Spicy sauce can make you tear up. High heat can make you sizzle. So, follow the recipe and use your brain. Don't mess up the dish. And wash your hands and stuff. You don't want to get dirty or sick. You have been warned.

Burgers are awesome and versatile - unlike some people I know. They are also great for sharing with friends, if you have any.

Burger

Ingredients:

- ◯ A burger patty. Meaty or not
- ◯ A burger bun. Seedy or not
- ◯ Some cheese. Melty or not
- ◯ Some lettuce. Leafy or not
- ◯ Some tomato. Juicy or not
- ◯ Some sauce. Saucy or not.

Items:

- ◯ Frying pan and stove
- ◯ Spatula
- ◯ Plate and knife

Instructions:

1. Heat the frying pan over medium-high heat. This will make it hot.
2. Cook the burger patty in the pan for about 4 minutes on each side, or until it's cooked to your liking. You can also add some salt, pepper, garlic powder, or any other seasoning you like. Don't overcook or undercook the patty. That's bad.
3. Add the cheese on top of the patty in the last minute of cooking.
4. Cut the burger bun in half with the knife. Be careful not to cut yourself.
5. Toast the bun halves in the same pan or in a toaster. This will make them warm and crispy.
6. Assemble the burger by placing the bottom bun on the plate, then the lettuce, then the tomato, then the cheese-topped patty, then the sauce, then the top bun.
7. Enjoy your burger. It's juicy, cheesy, and yummy. You can also share it with someone else. Or not. It's up to you.
8. Bite your burger and savor the flavors. You'll be happy and satisfied. You can also snap your burger and share it online. Your friends will be jealous and hungry.
9. Do step 8 until no burger left. You'll be full and content. You can also keep some for later or give some to others.

Warning

Burgers are tasty, but tricky. Watch the fillings, the heat, and the drip. Fillings can slip and slide. Heat can scald and sear. Drip can stain and smear. So, mind your burger and your clothes. Don't mess up your bite or your look. You have been warned.

"WHETHER IT'S A 10-MINUTE MIRACLE OR A SLOW-COOKED SENSATION, THESE EASY DISHES ARE YOUR SECRET WEAPONS FOR PROVING YOU'VE GOT THIS ADULTING THING DOWN—ONE DELICIOUS BITE AT A TIME!"

CHAPTER III
Hot Tips

Best before / Used by

Best before dates are like suggestions from your food. They tell you when your food will be at its peak quality and freshness, but they don't mean your food will go bad after that date. You can still eat your food after the best before date, as long as it looks, smells, and tastes okay. Just use your common sense and your senses. For example, you can still eat your yogurt a few days after the best before date, as long as it's not moldy or sour. But don't push your luck too much. You don't want to end up with a stomach ache or worse.

Used by dates are like commands from your food. They tell you when your food will be unsafe to eat and should be thrown away, no matter what. You should never eat your food after the used by date, even if it looks, smells, and tastes okay. You can't trust your common sense or your senses. For example, you should never eat your chicken a day after the used by date, even if it's not slimy or smelly. It could have harmful bacteria that can make you sick or worse.

So, the next time you're cooking, pay attention to the dates on your food.

Remember: best before dates are suggestions, used by dates are commands. Don't confuse them or ignore them. You have been warned.

Seasoning to taste

- **Taste buds don't lie:** The only way to know if your food is yummy is to taste it often. Just don't burn your tongue or drool into the pot. Adjust the seasoning as you go and avoid blandness or saltiness.

- **Less is more:** You can always add more seasoning, but you can't take it away. Unless you have a time machine or a magic wand. Use a pinch of salt, pepper, or other flavors and increase it gradually. You can also use low-sodium or unsalted ingredients to have more control.

- **Spice up your life:** Salt and pepper are fine, but they are not the only spices in the world. There are hundreds of herbs, spices, sauces, and other flavorings to choose from. You can use fresh or dried, depending on your mood and availability. Just remember to use more fresh than dried and add them at the end.

- **Flavor 101:** Different cuisines and dishes have different flavor profiles, which are like their personalities. For example, Italian food is friendly and cheerful, while Indian food is spicy and adventurous. Learn the basics of flavor combinations and you'll be able to create authentic and delicious dishes, or even your own recipes.

Spicing up your dish

- **Bell pepper:** The mildest of the bunch, these chillies are so sweet and bright, they're practically candy. They're perfect for stuffing, slicing, or snacking. Just don't expect any heat from them, unless you count the sunburn from their vibrant colours.
- **Jalapeño:** These chillies are the stars of Mexican cuisine, adding a tangy and spicy kick to salsas, guacamole, and nachos. They're also great for smoking and drying, becoming the smoky and rich chipotle chillies. Just be careful not to bite into a particularly hot one, or you'll be reaching for the nearest glass of milk.
- **Bird's eye:** These little chillies pack a punch in both flavour and heat. They're common in Southeast Asian cooking, where they're crushed, sliced, or whole in sauces, curries, and stir-fries. They're also known as Thai chillies, but don't let that fool you. They're not here to play nice, they're here to make you sweat.
- **Habanero:** These chillies are not for the faint of heart. They're among the hottest on the list, with a fruity and floral flavour that can create havoc in your mouth. They're often used to make hot sauces, but you can also use them in small amounts in other dishes. Just make sure you wear gloves when handling them, and don't touch your eyes or any other sensitive areas. Trust me, you don't want to find out what that feels like.
- **Cayenne:** These chillies are long, slim, and spicy, with an earthy and peppery flavour. They're often used in Cajun, Indian, and Chinese cuisines. They're also ground into a powder that can be used to season anything from popcorn to chocolate. Just don't go overboard with it, or you'll end up with a mouthful of fire.

What not do to!

- **Don't use your smoke alarm as a timer:** If you hear a loud beeping sound, it means your food is burning, not ready.
- **Don't confuse baking soda and baking powder:** They are not the same thing, and they will make your cake rise differently. Or explode.
- **Don't cut yourself:** This may seem obvious, but knives are sharp and fingers are not. Always use a cutting board, hold the knife firmly, and keep your fingers away from the blade.
- **Don't leave your food unattended:** Whether you are boiling, frying, or roasting, you need to keep an eye on your food. Otherwise, you may end up with a pot of mush, or a burnt down home.
- **Don't forget to wash your hands:** This is not only hygienic, but also prevents cross-contamination. You don't want to transfer bacteria, dirt, or flavors from one food to another.
- **Don't overcook your pasta:** Pasta should be cooked al dente, which means firm to the bite, not soft and mushy. To check if your pasta is done, taste it, don't throw it against the wall.
- **Don't microwave metal:** Metal objects, such as forks, spoons, or foil, can cause sparks, fires, or explosions in the microwave. Use microwave-safe containers and utensils, and remove any metal before heating your food.
- **Don't put hot oil in water:** Hot oil and water don't mix well. They can cause violent splashes, burns, or even fires. Let the oil cool down before disposing of it, or use a separate container.
- **Don't give up:** Cooking can be fun and rewarding, but also challenging and frustrating. You may make mistakes, but you can also learn from them. Don't be afraid to experiment, improvise, or ask for help. And remember, practice makes perfect.

Money saving tips

- **Bulk Up, Slim Down Your Bills:** Buy pasta, rice, and canned goods in bulk. Your pantry will look like a Costco, but your wallet will thank you!
- **Meal Ninja:** Plan meals ahead to avoid impulse buying. Plus, you'll feel like a food superhero with a plan!
- **Batch and Freeze, the Budget's BFF:** Cook in batches and freeze like you're stocking up for a culinary apocalypse.]
- **Loyalty Pays Off:** Use those loyalty cards like a pro. You might even earn enough points for a free snack!
- **Second-Hand, First Class:** Furnish your place with second-hand treasures. It's not just eco-friendly; it's budget-chic!
- **Energy Detective:** Be an energy-saving detective. Turn off lights, unplug devices, and watch your utility bills shrink like magic.
- **Roomie Revolution (but Worth It!):** Having a roommate cuts rent and expenses in half. Even if they eat your food and keep you up at night with their Netflix and chill, it's still a valuable deal!
- **Pay Your Future Self First:** Before splurging on that fancy coffee or avocado on toast, make like a time traveler and pay your future self first. Your future self will thank you for the surprise bonus!
- **Budget Boss:** Set a budget and stick to it!

CHAPTER IV
Your recipes

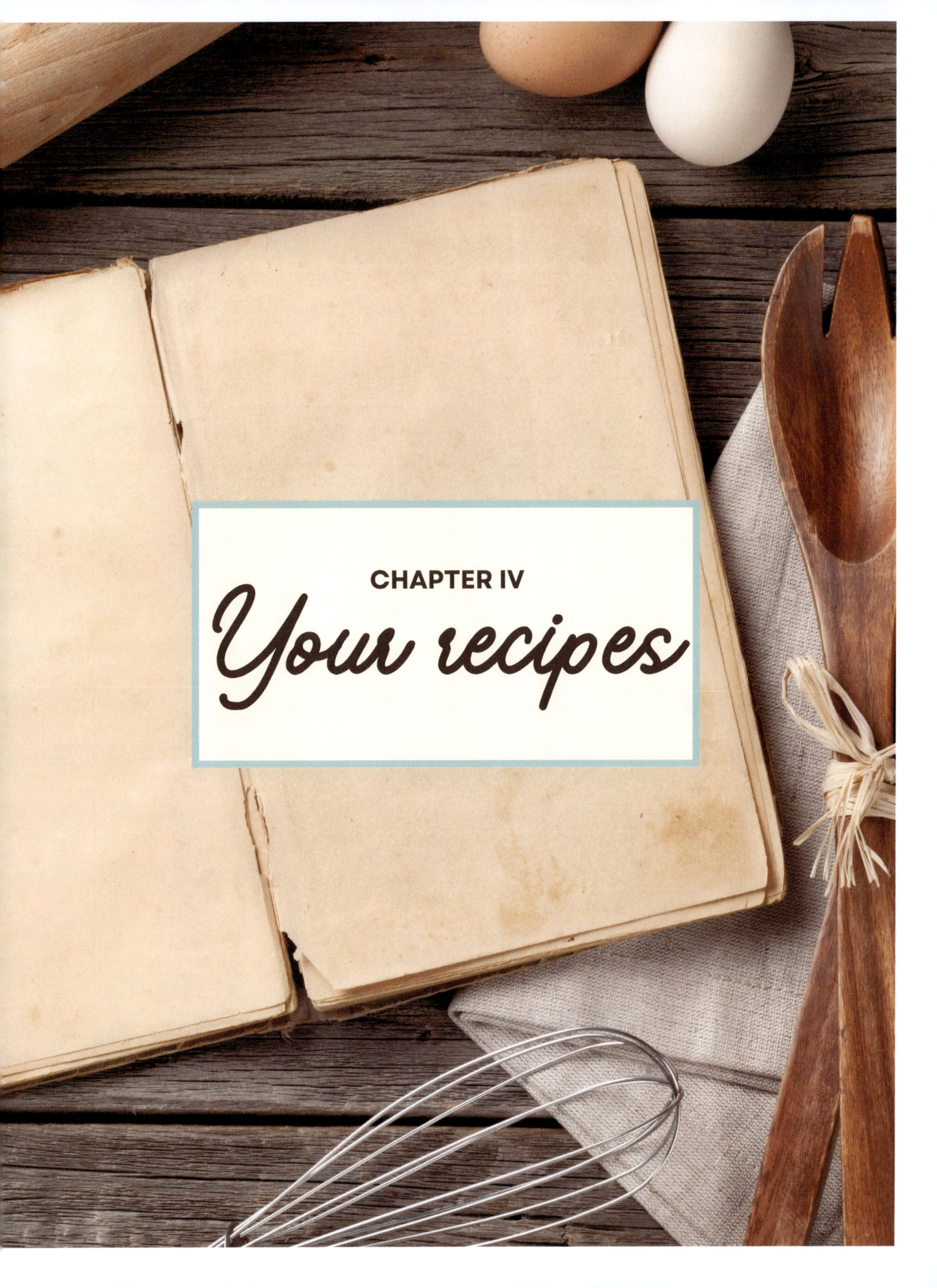

Title:

Ingredients:

Steps:

Title:

Ingredients:

Steps:

Title:

Ingredients:

Steps:

Title:

Ingredients:

Steps:

Title:

Ingredients:

Steps:

Title:

Ingredients:

Steps:

Title:

Ingredients:

Steps:

Title:

Ingredients:

Steps:

Title:

Ingredients:

Steps:

Title:

Ingredients:

Steps:

Title:

Ingredients:

Steps:

Title:

Ingredients:

Steps:

Title:

Ingredients:

Steps:

CHAPTER V
Notes

Notes

Notes

Notes

Notes

Notes

Notes

Notes

Notes

Notes

Notes

Notes

Notes

Notes

Notes

Notes

Notes

Notes

Notes

Printed in Great Britain
by Amazon